OVERCOMING
CREATIVE
ANXIETY

OVERCOMING CREATIVE ANXIETY

Journal Prompts &
Practices for Disarming
Your Inner Critic &
Allowing Creativity to Flow

KAREN C.L. ANDERSON

CORAL GABLES

For permission requests, please contact the publisher at:
Mango Publishing Group
2850 S Douglas Road, 2nd Floor
Coral Gables, FL 33134 USA
info@mango.bz

For special orders, quantity sales, course adoptions and corporate sales, please
email the publisher at sales@mango.bz. For trade and wholesale sales, please
contact Ingram Publisher Services at customer.service@ingramcontent.com or
+1.800.509.4887.

Overcoming Creative Anxiety: Journal Prompts & Practices for Disarming Your Inner
Critic & Allowing Creativity to Flow

Library of Congress Cataloging-in-Publication number: 2020933895
ISBN: (print) 978-1-64250-251-0, (ebook) 978-1-64250-252-7
BISAC category code SEL009000, SELF-HELP / Creativity

Printed in the United States of America

This book is dedicated to your fear

and your creativity.

Contents

Preface

"Do you have any interest in creating a journal on overcoming your Inner Critic?" read the email from my editor.

"Oh wow," I said to my husband. "I just got an email from my editor asking if I'd like to write about the Inner Critic. I can't do that. That's not my subject. They should ask [insert name of expert here] to write that book."

Those are the words that tumbled out of my mouth in that moment.

My husband looked at me incredulously, his eyebrows raised, as if to say, "You've got to be kidding me. You're the perfect person to write that book."

I'm going to let my Inner Advocate interject right here to let you know that the two sentences above were added to the manuscript after I submitted the first draft. My editor said she wanted more detail. I panicked a bit. And then I let myself follow my own advice regarding creativity. I typed some words, then deleted them. I got up to empty the dishwasher, a chore I detest. I came back. I typed some more words. Then I got up to get a snack even though I wasn't hungry. I came back and typed some more words. I looked up the definition of "critic" and the definition of "advocate." Then I played a round of Words with Friends. Came back to it. The more I typed and thought and noodled and deleted and typed and distracted myself, the more that feeling came over me...the feeling I know to be my Creative Self. The feeling that tells me I am onto something: a slight buzzing or quickening in my chest, an expansiveness. My eyes soften and sometimes I tear up. My limbs feel rubbery in a pleasant way. It's like I've surrendered to the process. And here's the thing: I get this feeling as I do my thing, not necessarily prior to doing it. I have to stumble and be awkward and make mistakes and let it be uncomfortable. And then...and then the "right" words come to me and I have a flurry of typing and my chest buzzes and my eyes soften and tear up and all is right with the world. **I am writing!**

Okay, where was I? Oh yeah, the email asking if I was interested in writing this book.

I let it sit in my inbox overnight.

The next morning, I chatted with a friend.

"So my editor reached out to me yesterday afternoon with a question that I am not sure how to answer… She asked if I am interested in writing a guided journal for overcoming the Inner Critic."

"Do you have any interest in that?" she asked.

"I do, but I don't really know anything about it. There are so many other people who are better suited for it…more qualified. Like [insert name of expert here]. Oh jeez, if I do this, will [insert name of expert here] think I'm stealing their ideas? Hasn't this subject been done to death? Yeah, I know, there are no new ideas, it's about what I bring to the subject. That's what creativity is, right? Taking an existing idea and putting through my process."

My friend looked at me the same way my husband had.

Creativity is the opposite of fear.

—Unknown

Here's the thing: I couldn't quite grasp that what had been asked of me was real. I was conscious of the fact that, hello, my Inner Critic was running the show and that I'd created (hint, hint) a fearful experience around this request.

Finally, I had a good laugh at myself and responded to the email:

"Yes, I'd love to create a journal on overcoming the Inner Critic! The reason I didn't respond right away is because I had to have a conversation with my Inner Critic. How meta."

※ ※ ※

You are creating right this very minute.

With every thought you think, you create literal vibrations or sensations in your body that your brain then translates and labels with words you know as emotions. In turn, your feelings cause you to act, react, shut down, open up, do, not do…and thus you create.

You create experiences based on the input your mind receives and then translates. Emotional experiences, active experiences, results-based experiences, relational experiences.

Creativity isn't only for art and music. Or technology and engineering. Or food. Or clothing. It's also for relationships and experiences.

So the good news is that you're already creative. You were born that way.

Here's the catch: you were also born with a fear-based "critic."

And the not-great (but good-to-know) news? It's easier to be critical than it is to be creative.

This is because the fear-based critical part of the human brain— evolution-wise—is much older and more experienced than the creative part.

✺ ✺ ✺

Your life is already artful, waiting, just
waiting, for you to make it art.

—Toni Morrison

✺ ✺ ✺

The fear-based critical part of your brain just does what it does and doesn't even have to "think" about it. The creative part, on the other hand, can be slower and bit more awkward. And the critical part doesn't like that. The critical part fears the unknown, and creativity is all about the unknown.

The best news of all? Your brain also includes an Inner Advocate. All that's required is your willingness and curiosity.

Your human brain was designed to create a whole and complete experience for you, and this includes your Inner Critic, your Inner Advocate, and your Creative Self.

In this journal you will find the writing prompts and practices I use to know and understand my Inner Critic, to cultivate my Inner Advocate, to remember and inspire my Creative Self.

Meet Your Inner Critic

Born from experiences internalized early in life, the Inner Critic an amalgamation of every critical thing we've ever heard (or thought we heard) from people of influence as they attempted to push us to conform to the norms of society.

—Denise Jacobs, author of *Banish Your Inner Critic*

Critic (noun): one given to harsh or captious judgment

"I'm a pathetic loser."

———

"No one wants what I have to offer."

———

"I'm not scholarly enough."

———

"I'm not compassionate enough."

———

"I don't have enough patience."

———

"I'm too easily distracted."

———

"I don't have any original ideas."

———

"I'm a spoiled brat."

———

"I'm lazy."

———

"I take the easy way out."

———

Pretty horrible, huh?

These are just a few of the things my Inner Critic serves up to me. To this day.

These words, phrases, and sentences are an amalgamation of all the critical things I've ever heard—or thought I've heard—from the people of influence in my life. They weren't necessarily said to me *about* me (although some of them were). In some cases, they were said and/or modeled by those people of influence *about themselves or others.*

What I've learned is that these words, phrases, and sentences are simply opinions and subjective judgments. They are not the truth (even though they often feel like the truth).

I used to be ruled by thoughts like these because I wasn't aware that I was actually thinking them. I lived my life as if they were the truth.

In this section you're going to get to meet and get to know your Inner Critic.

I could say, "Don't be afraid," but there's a good chance you are. Or at least uncomfortable. These feelings are not only okay, they're normal. Feel them and pick up your writing instrument anyway.

Who is your Inner Critic? Where did it come from?
Who are the "people of influence" in your life who make up
your Inner Critic?

_____

_____

_____

_____

_____

_____

_____

_____

_____

_____

_____

_____

_____

_____

_____

_____

_____

_____

_____

_____

Draw a picture, literally or with words, of your Inner Critic. Get really specific about what your Inner Critic looks and acts like.

Does your Inner Critic have a name? What is it?

_____

_____

_____

_____

_____

_____

~~Elaine~~

~~Big Meanie~~

~~Howard~~

~~Spencer~~

Describe your Inner Critic's voice. Don't write down what it says (we'll get to that); simply describe what it sounds like (tone, quality, volume, etc.) in as much detail as you can.

_____

_____

_____

_____

_____

_____

_____

_____

_____

_____

_____

_____

_____

_____

_____

_____

_____

_____

_____

_____

_____

Pretend you just met your Inner Critic at a networking event. Have it introduce itself to you and tell you what it believes its job is in your life.

What is your relationship to your Inner Critic?

_____
_____
_____
_____
_____
_____
_____
_____
_____
_____
_____
_____
_____
_____
_____
_____
_____
_____
_____
_____
_____

What is your Inner Critic trying to teach you?

_____

_____

_____

_____

_____

_____

_____

_____

_____

_____

_____

_____

_____

_____

_____

_____

_____

_____

_____

_____

_____

What is your Inner Critic trying to fix?

_____

_____

_____

_____

_____

_____

_____

_____

_____

_____

_____

_____

_____

_____

_____

_____

_____

_____

_____

_____

_____

_____

What is your Inner Critic trying to make perfect?

_____

_____

_____

_____

_____

_____

_____

_____

_____

_____

_____

_____

_____

_____

_____

_____

_____

_____

_____

_____

_____

＊ ＊ ＊

Perfection is just fear that you're not enough in pearls and a fancy mink coat. It tricks you into thinking it's a virtue. Its trick is that it tells you that it makes you special but really all its doing is stopping you from having a life that is rewarding and creative. It's not subtle. It only knows to tell you to stop when it doesn't know what the outcome will be. The more you fight it, the more it asserts itself. The higher part of your brain doesn't have the fuel that the older part does. Fear is way older than the prefrontal cortex. They don't know how to talk to each other. So we have to learn how to talk to our fears in a kind and loving way.

—Elizabeth Gilbert

＊ ＊ ＊

Complete this sentence:
"I know the Inner Critic has taken over when I..."

_____

_____

_____

_____

_____

_____

_____

_____

_____

_____

_____

_____

_____

_____

_____

_____

_____

_____

_____

_____

_____

What would you do if your Inner Critic hadn't told you what to do (or what it thinks is best)?

_____

_____

_____

_____

_____

_____

_____

_____

_____

_____

_____

_____

_____

_____

_____

_____

_____

_____

_____

_____

What is perfect about your Inner Critic?

_____

_____

_____

_____

_____

_____

_____

_____

_____

_____

_____

_____

_____

_____

_____

_____

_____

_____

_____

_____

_____

_____

_____

What is funny about your Inner Critic?

_____

_____

_____

_____

_____

_____

_____

_____

_____

_____

_____

_____

_____

_____

_____

_____

_____

_____

_____

_____

_____

_____

Take your Inner Critic for a fifteen-minute walk. When you get back, write about the experience. What did your Inner Critic notice on the walk? What comments did it have?

_____

_____

_____

_____

_____

_____

_____

_____

_____

_____

_____

_____

_____

_____

_____

_____

_____

_____

_____

_____

Write down everything your Inner Critic says to you, about you.

_____
_____
_____
_____
_____
_____
_____
_____
_____
_____
_____
_____
_____
_____
_____
_____
_____
_____
_____
_____
_____
_____
_____
_____

What does your Inner Critic believe about you? About others? About the world?

_____

_____

_____

_____

_____

_____

_____

_____

_____

_____

_____

_____

_____

_____

_____

_____

_____

_____

_____

_____

_____

_____

Completing these sentences can help you access your Inner Critic's beliefs:

"I fear..."

_____

_____

"The worst thing that could happen is..."

_____

_____

"I am ashamed when..."

_____

_____

"I feel stupid when..."

_____

_____

"I think I am incapable when..."

_____

_____

When you think about your Inner Critic and what it has to say, how do you feel? Get literal and granular with this one. Describe the sensations (tightening in the gut, clenched jaw, shallow breathing, heaviness in your chest, etc.) and the corresponding emotions (afraid, desperate, distressed, angry, frustrated, etc.). Where do you feel these sensations in your body? What color are they? Do they have a texture? A temperature? Some other quality? Do they change the more you focus on and describe them? How? Write it down or draw a picture. You could even lie down on a huge piece of paper and have someone draw an outline around you. Then fill in the places where each emotion resides and what it looks like. Use whatever media calls to you.

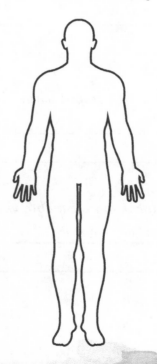

How much of what your Inner Critic says are truly indisputable facts that could be proven in a court of law? Be honest.

_____

_____

_____

_____

_____

_____

_____

_____

_____

_____

_____

_____

_____

_____

_____

_____

_____

_____

_____

✳ ✳ ✳

Self-doubt is proof of your humanity. Not your inadequacy.

—Tanya Geisler

Complete this sentence: "If I didn't have an Inner Critic, I'd..."

_____

_____

_____

_____

_____

_____

Or fill in the blanks:
"If I wasn't afraid to feel

_____

_____

_____ ,

I'd

_____

_____

_____

_____ ."

What is your biggest concern about your Inner Critic?

_____

_____

_____

_____

_____

_____

_____

_____

_____

_____

_____

_____

_____

_____

_____

_____

_____

_____

_____

_____

What surprises you the most about your Inner Critic?

_____

_____

_____

_____

_____

_____

_____

_____

_____

_____

_____

_____

_____

_____

_____

_____

_____

_____

_____

_____

_____

_____

Write down all the things your Inner Critic fears about what other people think.

_____

_____

_____

_____

_____

_____

_____

_____

_____

_____

_____

_____

_____

_____

_____

_____

_____

_____

_____

_____

_____

_____

What have you accomplished or achieved that was driven by your Inner Critic? In other words, it was out of fear of criticism that you _____.

_____

_____

_____

_____

_____

_____

_____

_____

_____

_____

_____

_____

_____

_____

_____

_____

_____

_____

_____

Have your Inner Critic write you a letter telling you what it needs and wants you to know.

_____

_____

_____

_____

_____

_____

_____

_____

_____

_____

_____

_____

_____

_____

_____

_____

_____

_____

_____

_____

_____

_____

_____

Interview your Inner Critic and then respond as your Inner Critic. Play both roles. What do you say/ask/do?

_____

_____

_____

_____

_____

_____

_____

_____

_____

_____

_____

_____

_____

_____

_____

_____

_____

_____

_____

_____

_____

_____

What permission do you need from your Inner Critic?

_____

_____

_____

_____

_____

_____

_____

_____

_____

_____

_____

_____

_____

_____

_____

_____

_____

_____

_____

_____

_____

What might you accept about yourself so your Inner Critic can no longer use it to diminish (or manipulate) you?

_____

_____

_____

_____

_____

_____

_____

_____

_____

_____

_____

_____

_____

_____

_____

_____

_____

_____

_____

_____

_____

What are you willing to delegate to your Inner Critic to keep it
occupied while you go forth and create?

_____

_____

_____

_____

_____

_____

_____

_____

_____

_____

_____

_____

_____

_____

_____

_____

_____

_____

_____

_____

_____

Complete this sentence: it is now safe for me to...

_____

_____

_____

_____

_____

_____

Acknowledging your fear-based Inner Critic calms it down, dissolves any resistance it has, and makes a distinction between the past and right now.

P.S. Trying to get rid of your Inner Critic is like trying to get rid of your humanity.

※ ※ ※

We've been conditioned to think we shouldn't have
an Inner Critic and that it's bad and we're doomed if
we do. That's not the case. Your Inner Critic is simply
an indicator that you need your own attention.

—Nicole Lewis-Keeber

※ ※ ※

Somatic Practice

One

Affirm yourself and your presence.

"I am here.

My name is _____.
It is [date, time] and I am here at [location]."

Notice how it feels in your body to do this. Try it standing up and see how it changes. Notice what your body wants to do as you affirm yourself and your presence.

Cultivate Your

Inner Advocate

Be brave and curious, not fearful and suspicious...

—Eddie Izzard

Advocate (noun): one who writes or speaks in support or defense of another; a protector, champion, cheerleader

---

"I've got this."

———

"I have all the time in the world."

———

"I do it my way."

———

*"I **get** to do it my way."*

———

"My process is my process for a reason...it's mine."

———

"I can do hard things without suffering (too much)."

———

"I give myself the time and space to create."

———

"I am an example of what is possible."

———

"I am a writer."

———

"I believe in you when you can't believe in yourself."

———

These are the things my Inner Advocate says to me. Unlike the things my Inner Critic says, it's harder to remember these words, phrases, and sentences because my brain is hardwired for negativity (and so is yours). It is simply easier to be negative and to find evidence to support it.

Also, just as there are the people of influence who said and modeled the things that now inform your Inner Critic, people of influence also said and modeled things that can inform your Inner Advocate. It goes both ways.

Like the things my Inner Critic says, these words, phrases, and sentences are opinions and subjective judgments. They are not necessarily true (for example, I don't have all the time in the world). But here's the part to pay close attention to: unlike what the Inner Critic says, *what my Inner Advocate says feels good when I choose to believe it.* These words, phrases, and sentences support me in doing the things I say I want to do.

In this section, you're going to meet and get to know your Inner Advocate. Ready?

Make a list of people who could make up your Inner Advocate. They could be living or dead. Real or fictional. Why did you choose them? What qualities and values do they represent? Who are/were the people in your life who cheered you on?

_____

_____

_____

_____

_____

_____

_____

_____

_____

_____

_____

_____

_____

_____

_____

_____

_____

_____

_____

Draw a picture, literally or with words, of your Inner Advocate. Get really specific about what your Inner Advocate looks and acts like.

Describe your Inner Advocate's voice. Don't write down what it says, simply describe what it sounds like (tone, quality, volume, etc.) in as much detail as you can.

_____

_____

_____

_____

_____

_____

_____

_____

_____

_____

_____

_____

_____

_____

_____

_____

_____

_____

_____

_____

_____

How might your Inner Advocate help you detach, mentally and emotionally, from your Inner Critic and its stories and beliefs?

_____

_____

_____

_____

_____

_____

_____

_____

_____

_____

_____

_____

_____

_____

_____

_____

_____

_____

_____

_____

_____

_____

What do you need from your Inner Advocate?

_____

_____

_____

_____

_____

_____

_____

_____

_____

_____

_____

_____

_____

_____

_____

_____

_____

_____

_____

_____

_____

_____

Take your Inner Advocate for a fifteen-minute walk. When you get back, write about the experience. What did your Inner Advocate notice on the walk? What comments did it have? How was this fifteen-minute walk different than the walk you took with your Inner Critic?

_____

_____

_____

_____

_____

_____

_____

_____

_____

_____

_____

_____

_____

_____

_____

_____

_____

_____

_____

_____

What does your Inner Advocate believe about you?
About others? About the world?

_____

_____

_____

_____

_____

_____

_____

_____

_____

_____

_____

_____

_____

_____

_____

_____

_____

_____

_____

_____

_____

_____

_____

Completing these sentences can help you access your Inner Advocate's beliefs:

"I love..."

_____

_____

"The best thing that could happen is..."

_____

_____

"I feel amazing when..."

_____

_____

"I feel good when..."

_____

_____

"I think I am my best self when..."

_____

_____

When you think about your Inner Advocate and what it has to say, how do you feel? Get literal and granular with this one. Describe the sensations (expansiveness in your chest, soft eyes, tingling in your tummy, energy, etc.) and corresponding emotions (loved, alive, calm, excited, thrilled, giddy, etc.). Where do you feel these sensations in your body? What color are they? Do they have a texture? A temperature? Some other quality? Do they change the more you focus on and describe them? How? Write it down or draw a picture. You could even lie down on a huge piece of paper and have someone draw an outline around you. Then fill in the places where each emotion resides and what it looks like. Use whatever media calls to you.

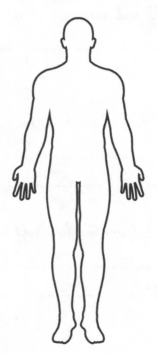

_____

_____

_____

_____

_____

_____

_____

_____

_____

_____

_____

_____

_____

_____

_____

_____

_____

_____

_____

_____

_____

_____

_____

_____

_____

Complete this sentence:
"I know my Inner Advocate has my back when I..."

_____

_____

_____

_____

_____

_____

_____

_____

_____

_____

_____

_____

_____

_____

_____

_____

_____

_____

_____

_____

_____

_____

What wisdom does your Inner Critic have for your Inner Advocate?

_____

_____

_____

_____

_____

_____

_____

_____

_____

_____

_____

_____

_____

_____

_____

_____

_____

_____

_____

_____

_____

_____

What wisdom does your Inner Advocate have for your Inner Critic?

_____

_____

_____

_____

_____

_____

_____

_____

_____

_____

_____

_____

_____

_____

_____

_____

_____

_____

_____

_____

What can your Inner Advocate tell your Inner Critic about how to be brave and big in the world?

_____

_____

_____

_____

_____

_____

_____

_____

_____

_____

_____

_____

_____

_____

_____

_____

_____

_____

_____

_____

What kind of relationship does your Inner Advocate have with your Inner Critic?

_____

_____

_____

_____

_____

_____

_____

_____

_____

_____

_____

_____

_____

_____

_____

_____

_____

_____

_____

_____

_____

_____

How might your Inner Advocate model to your Inner Critic
what it looks like to be confident?

_____

_____

_____

_____

_____

_____

_____

_____

_____

_____

_____

_____

_____

_____

_____

_____

_____

_____

_____

_____

_____

Pay attention to the times when you feel pathetic, unlovable, disgusting, empty, needy, stupid, ignorant, helpless, and incapable. In those moments, call on your Inner Advocate and ask it for advice. What does it say? How does it say it? What tone of voice does your Inner Advocate use? How does it look at you?

_____

_____

_____

_____

_____

_____

_____

_____

_____

_____

_____

_____

_____

_____

_____

_____

_____

_____

_____

What thoughts does your Inner Advocate think and practice on purpose?

How can your Inner Advocate create distance between you and your Inner Critic?

_____

_____

_____

_____

_____

_____

_____

_____

_____

_____

_____

_____

_____

_____

_____

_____

_____

_____

_____

_____

What's more important to you: your Creative Self's intentions or your Inner Critic's opinions? Why? You can continue to reject the Inner Critic, but is it in service to your intention?

_____

_____

_____

_____

_____

_____

_____

_____

_____

_____

_____

_____

_____

_____

_____

_____

_____

_____

_____

What words do you associate with your Inner Advocate? Here are some that may resonate. Add your own.

- rest
- time
- choice
- kindness
- attention
- patience
- adjustment
- environment
- mindfulness
- gentle
- community
- process
- prioritizing
- slowing down
- exploration
- pleasure
- awareness

- acceptance
- support
- presence
- curiosity
- fascination
- _____
- _____
- _____
- _____
- _____
- _____
- _____
- _____
- _____
- _____
- _____

- _____
- _____
- _____
- _____
- _____
- _____
- _____
- _____
- _____
- _____
- _____
- _____
- _____
- _____
- _____
- _____
- _____

Your Inner Critic just said

_____

_____

In the past you reacted by

_____

_____

How does your Inner Advocate want to respond?

_____

_____

_____

_____

_____

_____

_____

_____

_____

_____

_____

_____

_____

_____

When your Inner Critic shows up, you tend to abandon yourself.
Make a list of ways you abandon yourself.

_____

_____

_____

_____

_____

_____

_____

_____

_____

_____

_____

_____

_____

_____

_____

_____

_____

_____

_____

Ask your Inner Advocate to tell you how to bring yourself
back to you.

_____

_____

_____

_____

_____

_____

_____

_____

_____

_____

_____

_____

_____

_____

_____

_____

_____

_____

_____

_____

_____

_____

Ask your Inner Advocate to tell you the difference between your intuition and your Inner Critic.

_____

_____

_____

_____

_____

_____

_____

_____

_____

_____

_____

_____

_____

_____

_____

_____

_____

_____

_____

_____

Ask your Inner Advocate to tell your Inner Critic how it knows
you are safe and that it is safe to create.

_____

_____

_____

_____

_____

_____

_____

_____

_____

_____

_____

_____

_____

_____

_____

_____

_____

_____

_____

_____

_____

Nothing I accept about myself can be
used against me to diminish me.

—Audre Lord

❋ ❋ ❋

Somatic Practice

Two

Orient yourself.

Sit as comfortably as you can and let your attention wander around your space. Notice what attracts your attention and draws your interest. Pick three things and say (out loud or inside your head) each thing as your eyes focus on it.

Then move your attention inward and notice what attracts your attention there. Notice sensations: urges to move, tightness, softness, pressure, etc. Name them and see how they evolve.

Don't judge your observations. Simply make a note of them. In this way, you will establish yourself in the here and now.

Pop Quiz

Just the facts: go back and read everything your Inner Critic says and then pull out just the facts. For the purposes of this exercise, facts are things that every person would agree to; facts are what can be proven in a court of law.

Fact:
You are a
human being.

Not fact:
You can't do
anything right.

How much of what you Inner Critic says is fact?
Remember this: everything else is opinion, judgment, thoughts,
beliefs, but not facts. In other words, it's optional.

_____

_____

_____

_____

_____

_____

_____

_____

_____

_____

_____

_____

_____

_____

_____

_____

_____

_____

For everything your Inner Critic says, ask yourself: do I want to believe it? If yes, why? If no, what do you want to believe instead?

_____

_____

_____

_____

_____

_____

_____

_____

_____

_____

_____

_____

_____

_____

_____

_____

_____

_____

_____

_____

_____

_____

Next to each statement, write down IC (for Inner Critic) or IA (for Inner Advocate) for which is most likely to say this to you.

I can't believe I failed again!

_____

I'm proud of myself for trying again...and again...and again...and again.[1]

_____

I'm hopeless!

_____

For God's sake, just do it!

_____

I will feel proud of myself when this is done.

_____

It will never work out.

_____

Is this possible?

_____

~~~~~

1. Thank you, Diane Nyad.

What was I thinking? Obviously, I wasn't!

_____

How can I turn this around?

_____

I can never catch a break.

_____

How can I give myself a break?

_____

I'm soooooo stupid!

_____

Why am I choosing to think that?

_____

It shouldn't have been that way.

_____

What would it feel like to accept that it was that way?

_____

Is there a gift in what happened?

_____

❋ ❋ ❋

It's easier to be a critic, than a creator.

—Nathan Myhrvold

❋ ❋ ❋

Somatic Practice

Three

Hold yourself.

This is a way to define your literal boundaries, and it has a calming effect on the nervous system.

Stand comfortably and place your hands on either side of your head. You can apply a bit of pressure or not. Imagine that you are molding a container for your thoughts. Feel the sensations in both your head and your hands.

Now move one hand to your forehead and the other to the back of your skull. Continue to notice the sensations and boundaries your hands are creating.

Move the hand on the back of your head to your heart and keep the other hand on your forehead. What changes? Are there sensations between your two hands?

Now move the hand that was on your forehead to your belly and keep the other hand on your heart. Continue to feel and notice the sensations.

And finally, move one hand to your solar plexus and one to the base of your head, where your head and neck meet and continue to observe.

Remember Your Creative Self

✻ ✻ ✻

We forget and remember
And we forget again
But this life is a circle
And it's coming back around
Coming back again

—Trevor Hall, "Bowl of Light"

✻ ✻ ✻

When I was a child, I dreamt of standing on a stage in a fabulous dress. I'd belt out a song that would make people weep with joy and get goosebumps. Without knowing it by these words, what I wanted was to make people feel and recognize their own humanity.

Alas, singing was not to be my creative outlet (at least not on public stages). But…but! I noticed that when I shared my writing in public, it had the same effect. The frisson of creative excitement I felt as I was writing seemed to land with others when I shared my writing and was then reflected back to me. I literally feel the energy flowing through me onto the page, into the hearts of my readers, and back to me again.

And then one day, after standing on a stage and telling a story, someone in the audience came up to me and said, "You made me recognize my own humanity."

Whoa.

I call this feeling Elemental Aliveness: an expansive buzzing or quickening in my chest, a softening of my eyes, a looseness in my limbs. There's a tension to it and, while it feels good, it's also a little uncomfortable. I've learned to love this feeling.

As you go through this next set of prompts, think about what creativity feels like (literally) for you, and what you might choose to call that feeling.

When do you feel most like yourself?

_____

_____

_____

_____

_____

_____

_____

_____

_____

_____

_____

_____

_____

_____

_____

_____

_____

_____

_____

_____

_____

_____

What is true for you in this moment?

_____

_____

_____

_____

_____

_____

_____

_____

_____

_____

_____

_____

_____

_____

_____

_____

_____

_____

_____

_____

What are the conditions that bring out your creativity?

_____

_____

_____

_____

_____

_____

_____

_____

_____

_____

_____

_____

_____

Creativity is the process of summoning feelings in your body on purpose so you can wield them intentionally in service to what you say you want.

What supports your creativity?

_____

_____

_____

_____

_____

_____

_____

_____

_____

_____

_____

_____

_____

_____

_____

_____

_____

_____

_____

_____

_____

※ ※ ※

What would you attempt if you knew you could not fail?

—Robert H. Schuller

※ ※ ※

What do you want to believe about yourself in regards to being creative?

_____

_____

_____

_____

_____

_____

_____

_____

_____

_____

_____

_____

_____

_____

_____

_____

_____

_____

_____

_____

_____

How do you want to feel?

_____

_____

_____

_____

_____

_____

_____

_____

_____

_____

_____

_____

_____

_____

_____

_____

_____

_____

_____

_____

_____

_____

How can you have more fun?

_____

_____

_____

_____

_____

_____

_____

_____

_____

_____

_____

_____

_____

_____

_____

_____

_____

_____

_____

_____

Why are you so lucky?

_____

_____

_____

_____

_____

_____

_____

_____

_____

_____

_____

_____

_____

_____

_____

_____

_____

_____

_____

_____

_____

_____

How would you like to feel on the other side of having created?

_____

_____

_____

_____

_____

_____

_____

_____

_____

_____

_____

_____

_____

_____

_____

_____

_____

_____

_____

_____

_____

What's worth doing even if you fail?

—Brené Brown

Take your Creative Self for a fifteen-minute walk. When you get back, write about the experience. What did your Creative Self notice on the walk? What comments did it have? How was this walk different than the walks you took with your Inner Advocate and Inner Critic?

_____

_____

_____

_____

_____

_____

_____

_____

_____

_____

_____

_____

_____

_____

_____

_____

_____

_____

_____

_____

How can you remember that you are creative?

_____

_____

_____

_____

_____

_____

_____

_____

_____

_____

_____

_____

_____

_____

_____

_____

_____

_____

_____

_____

✻ ✻ ✻

Your job isn't to stop forgetting, it's to keep remembering.

—Christie Inge

✻ ✻ ✻

Picture a time when you felt alive and on-purpose and in the flow. What were you doing? Who were you with? What else was happening? What did you believe and feel? Immerse yourself and all your senses in that moment and describe what it was like in as much detail as possible.

_____

_____

_____

_____

_____

_____

_____

_____

_____

_____

_____

_____

_____

_____

_____

_____

_____

_____

_____

Now, as you did with your Inner Critic and your Inner Advocate, write about how it literally feels when you are your Creative Self. Get literal and granular with this one. Describe the sensations and corresponding emotions. Where do you feel these sensations in your body? What color are they? Do they have a texture? A temperature? Some other quality? Do they change the more you focus on and describe them? How? Write it down or draw a picture. You could even lie down on a huge piece of paper and have someone draw an outline around you. Then fill in the places where each emotion resides and what it looks like. Use whatever media calls to you.

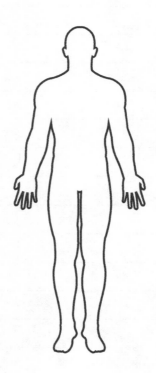

When I am in my creative flow, it feels like...

_____

_____

And I call it...

_____

_____

It is now safe for me to believe...

_____

_____

It is now safe for me to identify as...

_____

_____

It is now safe for me to...

_____

_____

✺ ✺ ✺

Go the limits of your longing... Flare up like flame and make
big shadows that I can move in. Let everything happen to
you: beauty and terror. Just keep going. No feeling is final.

—Rainer Maria Rilke

✺ ✺ ✺

Somatic Practice

Four

Express yourself.

This is a combination breathing exercise and chant, much like the "Om" in yoga. The vibrations created when you sound or chant a deep "voo" (on the exhale) "tone" the vagus nerve. The longest nerve in your body, the vagus nerve has two main functions: first, it monitors all the major organs in your body and communicates with the brain stem, and second, it regulates social engagement, digestion, alertness/consciousness, and emotions.

To practice, inhale through your nose and, as you exhale, make the "voo" sound (imagine a foghorn) in as low a tone as you can, making the effort to feel the vibrations in your lower abdomen.

After each round, close your eyes and sit calmly, noticing what you feel in your body.

Inspire Yourself

Wisdom begins in wonder.

—Socrates

The word "inspire" means "to breathe in." It also means to fill with the urge or ability to do or feel something, especially something creative.

Inspiration = breathing life into. In other words, inspiration doesn't come from out there; it's something you create. (Yeah, I know.)

When you're afraid, stressed, concerned, worried, and distracted (even if you're not fully aware of it), your breathing tends to be shallow and your creativity is blunted.

When you're relaxed, content, and curious, you breathe deeply… You breathe life into yourself and the projects, relationships, and experiences that excite and thrill you.

What are you breathing life into?

_____

_____

_____

_____

_____

_____

_____

_____

_____

_____

_____

_____

_____

_____

_____

_____

_____

_____

_____

_____

Creativity is necessary and has needs.

—Jonathan Tilley

In his TEDx talk, "What Creativity Is Trying to Tell You," Tilley says that creativity starts with an idea, and that it needs three things:

First it needs energetic and physical space:

> Energetic space might look like unscheduled time to do nothing but to sit with and noodle on your idea. It might look like you're doing nothing (and your Inner Critic won't like that at all). Let yourself be bored. Let yourself think; let your mind wander. Then bring back again to your idea.

> Physical space might be a studio or office. It might be the library or a coffee shop. Pay attention to how you feel in the space and ask yourself if it supports your creativity.

Second it needs mistakes:

> It needs to be played and grappled with, to be molded and shaped (a.k.a. "the messy middle"). It needs you to try this and that and the other thing. Sometimes it's about starting over and being willing to burn down a first draft.

> Don't let your Inner Critic stop you in this crucial phase of creativity. It's often uncomfortable, but it's also where the magic happens.

And third, it needs to be shared, to be released out into the world.

> Maybe you share with your friends first. Maybe you choose to share via social media. Maybe you start a blog or a YouTube channel. Find a way to share what you've created and don't let your Inner Critic stop you.

Here are some other ways to inspire yourself:

* **Make a playlist of songs/videos that help you feel creative.**

Here are three of my favorites; when I watch them, I feel elementally alive.

- "Lady Gaga singing to Sting at Kennedy Center Honors"
- "The Rockin' 1000 Singing 'Learn to Fly' "
- "Eddie Vedder singing 'Better Man' on David Letterman"

* **Sing along.**

* **Dance along.**

* **Let yourself feel whatever emotions come to the surface.**

* **Give yourself permission to have procrastination and distraction be part of your process.**

* **Revisit the prompts in this journal that resonate most.**

See what changes. Be curious.

* Use the four Somatic Practices.

They will help your nervous system regulate overwhelm or shut down. These simple practices can expand the capacity of your nervous system and cue your Inner Critic to know that it is safe.

* Create (see what I did there) distance from Inner Critic thoughts.

Use a technique described by physician and therapist Russ Harris in his book *The Happiness Trap*.

Pick a thought that you think often and usually bothers or upsets you. Mine is "I'm a pathetic loser."

Take that thought and, in front of it, insert this phrase:

"I am having the thought that...I'm a pathetic loser."

Then do it again, adding:

"I am noticing that I am having the thought that...I'm a pathetic loser."

And finally:

"How interesting...I am noticing that I am having the thought that...I'm a pathetic loser."

Notice what happens with each iteration.

The ability to observe yourself and your thoughts is powerful, and you are worthy of your own attention. And it's an ongoing practice.

✺ ✺ ✺

I am not the things my family did
I am not the voices in my head
I am not the pieces of the brokenness inside
I am light, I am light
I'm not the mistakes that I have made
or any of the things that caused me pain
I am not the pieces of the dream I left behind
I am light, I am light.

—India Arie

✺ ✺ ✺

Resources

The work of Tanya Geisler (tanyageisler.com)

"What Creativity Is Trying to Tell You," a TEDx talk by Jonathan Tilley (jonathantilley.com/speaking)

Other TED talks on creativity (ted.com/search?q=creativity)

Big Magic, a book by Elizabeth Gilbert (elizabethgilbert.com/books/big-magic)

The Creative Brain, a Netflix documentary (netflix.com/title/81090128)

Essentialism, a book by Greg McKeown (gregmckeown.com)

The Artist's Way, a book by Julia Cameron (juliacameronlive.com)

Banish Your Inner Critic, a book by Denise Jacobs (denisejacobs.com)

Somatic practices courtesy of the Somatic Experiencing Trauma Institute (traumahealing.org)

Acknowledgments

Gratitude to the team at Mango, especially my editor, Brenda Knight, who knew my Inner Critic wouldn't win; to Tanya Geisler who guided me in discovering Elemental Aliveness; to my friend Christie Inge, who asks me all the right questions; and always to my husband and partner in life Tim Anderson, who is one of the most creative people I know.

About the Author

Karen C.L. Anderson is the international bestselling author of several books with really long titles: *Dear Adult Daughter (With the Emphasis on Adult), Difficult Mothers, Adult Daughters: A Guide for Separation, Liberation & Inspiration* and *The Difficult Mother-Daughter Relationship Journal: A Guide for Revealing & Healing Toxic Generational Patterns*. She works with women on revealing and healing their difficult mother-daughter relationship stories and is writing a memoir, *A Letter to the Daughter I Chose Not to Have*.

She lives in Southeastern Connecticut.

Thank You

Stay in touch by signing up for my weekly Love Notes (answers to your questions, advice, essays, excerpts from books, offers, and other bits of wisdom delivered to your inbox every Thursday).

www.kclanderson.com/subscribe

Contact Information:

Agent:

Waterside Productions Inc.
2055 Oxford Ave.
Cardiff, CA 92007
Phone: 760-632-9190
Email: admin@waterside.com

Publisher:

Mango Media
2850 Douglas Road, Suite 201
Coral Gables, FL 33134
Phone: 305-428-2299
Email: support@mango.bz

Me:

Website: kclanderson.com
Facebook: facebook.com/KarenCLAnderson
Instagram: KCLAnderson

Mango Publishing, established in 2014, publishes an eclectic list of books by diverse authors—both new and established voices—on topics ranging from business, personal growth, women's empowerment, LGBTQ studies, health, and spirituality to history, popular culture, time management, decluttering, lifestyle, mental wellness, aging, and sustainable living. We were recently named 2019's #1 fastest growing independent publisher by *Publishers Weekly*. Our success is driven by our main goal, which is to publish high quality books that will entertain readers as well as make a positive difference in their lives.

Our readers are our most important resource; we value your input, suggestions, and ideas. We'd love to hear from you—after all, we are publishing books for you!

Please stay in touch with us and follow us at:
Facebook: Mango Publishing
Twitter: @MangoPublishing
Instagram: @MangoPublishing
LinkedIn: Mango Publishing
Pinterest: Mango Publishing

Sign up for our newsletter at www.mangopublishinggroup.com and receive a free book!

Join us on Mango's journey to reinvent publishing, one book at a time.